# The Death of
# Sportsmanship

## *And How to Revive It*

### Brian Shulman
*With Ragan Ingram*

LEARNING
THROUGH SPORTS™
*Great Students • Good Sports*

*The Death of Sportsmanship*
*And How to Revive It*
Copyright ©2007 by Brian Shulman

**Learning Through Sports**
5511 Highway 280 East, Suite 308
Birmingham, Alabama 35242
(205) 980-8970
www.learningthroughsports.com

Cover design: TLT Medis / Jillian Potter and Blake Johnson
Book design & production: Mike Brechner / Cypress House

ISBN 978-0-9791231-1-5

Printed in Canada
2 4 6 8 9 7 5 3 1

 This book is printed on recycled, acid-free paper containing 100% post-consumer waste recycled fiber.

# Acknowledgments

I have been blessed to have been surrounded by supportive family and friends. It started with my father, Stan, my mother, Joyce, and my sister Deborah. The happiness I enjoy today is a direct result of their guidance and love while I was growing up.

Coaches have had a tremendous influence in my life as well. Gene Andrews was like a second father to me in high school and beyond. Coach A, you'll never know how much it meant to me that you took the time to come up to Green Bay during training camp. For the short time that I was at the University of Tennessee, I had the opportunity to be around Coach George Cafego. He taught his players a lot more about life than kicking.

When I arrived at Auburn, I was mentored by former Auburn punter Alan Bollinger. The Auburn family may never know how much Alan influenced several of the greatest kickers and punters in Auburn football history. He's a great family man, and I appreciate the sacrifices he made on my behalf. I could not have stepped onto the field at Auburn without his teaching. Coach Dye, Coach Waldrop, and Coach Paul Davis are some of the greatest coaches, teachers, and leaders of men that this country has ever seen. They truly care about the person inside the uniform.

I would put all of my kids in any of these coaches' hands and know that they'd become successful and productive adults. For anyone reading this, I hope your kids have an opportunity to be around these kinds of men.

The same goes for the folks we interviewed. They all took time to provide their wisdom for this book; many are our partners, and have had tremendous influence on our company as well as on my life. I'm truly thankful for your willingness to share and help us achieve success more quickly. We all share the same goals and values.

I appreciate the friendship and talent of Ragan Ingram, who took my thoughts and brought them to life on the page. Thank you, Ragan!

Thanks to David Azbell, a true Alabama fan and State of Alabama man, for the title of this book. Laura LeNoir, you're a gem. Thanks for your wonderful attitude. You make coming to the office a joy every day.

My children, Tyler, Lauren, and Cole, are the reason why this book was created. Without seeing life through their eyes, I'm not sure I'd have noticed just how important sportsmanship is, and more important, how dead it's becoming.

My wife, Lisa, is an angel. She's the best mother and the most supportive wife in the world. I thank God for her and for our children. God led me to this journey, and I'm doing my best to follow His will daily. I am a very blessed man.

I hope this book and the work we do with our company will help change some lives.

*Brian Shulman, 2006*

---

I'm involved in this project because Brian Shulman has made it his life's work to make the games fun again for our youth and for adults. I admire his immense dedication to that effort, and appreciate the opportunity to help him with this project.

Sports have meant so much to me because my father threw hundreds of passes and shagged scores of fly balls through my childhood. He also taught me to write about them by sitting with me at a manual typewriter, composing stories of the games in which my older brother had played. My mother patiently washed uniforms for her three children for more than twenty years. My parents taught me that the games were to be fun, but that the friendships built and lessons learned would be better for me in the long run. I was blessed along the way to have many coaches who understood what sports were supposed to be and what they could be. None was better than Gene Hawkins, my first youth-league baseball coach. When I see him today, I can't help but want to dig in and try a little harder, knowing that he's pulling for me.

As an adult, I've been blessed with my wife, Karen, who has tolerated me through the sports-writing years, the officiating years, and now in my fan-in-the-stands years. She's learned to like the games, too, perhaps out of necessity. My children, Bo and Ali, have showered me with a lifetime of wonderful memories — on the field of play and beyond.

Most of all, I thank my Lord, Jesus Christ, who inspired the Apostle Paul to cite sports as a worthy teaching tool:

*Do you not know that those who run in a race all run, but one receives the prize? Run in such a way that you may obtain it. And everyone who competes for the prize is temperate in all things. Now they do it to obtain a perishable crown, but we for an imperishable crown. Therefore I run thus: not with uncertainty. Thus I fight: not as one who beats the air. But I discipline my body and bring it into subjection, lest, when I have preached to others, I myself should become disqualified.*

1 Corinthians 9:24–27 (New King James Version)

*Ragan Ingram, 2006*

# Preface

Think back to your first memory of your favorite sport. Seriously, take a minute and really think about it. Maybe it was playing catch with your dad, shooting hoops with your brothers, or trying to hit the tennis ball with your mom. For me it was football and Saturday mornings in Nashville, Tennessee, and the smell of freshly mowed grass. My father would drive me to the games, and I would have the best time of my life. I don't remember how many games we won, how many touchdowns I scored, or the number of tackles I made. All I remember is how much *fun* it was.

Society as it is now — and, more frightening, as it will become if our value system continues to suffer — needs a book like this one. Lately, the way we play our games has become an exposition of certain problems saturating our society. No one can deny that sportsmanship, if not dead, is seriously ill.

We need the discussion in this book in order to realize that there is something inarguably wrong with the trash-talking, fighting, vanity, disrespect, and the win-at-all-costs mentality that pervade today's sports, both professional and amateur. We need the discussion in this book to exhort us to remember the life lessons rewarded by sports when they're played as they were intended to be played since their inception — as a team, as a brotherhood, and for a common goal.

Most important, we need this discussion so that we can incite a return to the good of sports, for the good of our youth and future generations. This return will require the combined efforts of parents, coaches, educators, and even the media. I hope that you'll be stirred, because this change will require contributions from all of us — you, too, are a worthy voice in the response to poor sportsmanship.

Think of the reward we experience when sports are played on the foundations of brotherhood, mutual respect, and achievement through practice. We begin to appreciate the capabilities of our minds and bodies, we find companionship with those who give their all to the team, and we develop strong regard for those who teach us the rules and strategies of the game. We begin to have fun again! We all experience that reward, whether we're playing, coaching, supporting, or just watching.

As a society, we must remember the fundamental truth that sports — and all team activities — are about respect for each other as comrades, the complementary parts of the whole that we're so grateful to belong to. Sports are about human interaction, not individual egos or heroes. A great deal of pressure is taken off athletes, especially young athletes, when the focus returns to the team and the game, and the spotlight is removed from the showoff, the trash-talker, the cheater, and the poor sport.

When we accomplish a dimming of the limelight, sports become more than just entertainment and sensationalism; they become something we can all enjoy again, whether we're natural athletes or true spectators, and they become a positive instructional force in the lives of our youth.

The principle of observational learning says that youth will emulate the actions of others, especially those they consider role models. Professional and collegiate athletes and coaches can't escape the fact that these impressionable young minds study their actions and are highly likely to adopt the same behaviors they see while watching sports.

While some athletes and coaches argue that responsibility for character building and setting a good example belongs to parents, the media's constant coverage of sports figures and their antics makes it impossible for youth to ignore the personalities they're bombarded with as models of behavior.

The media isn't the only culprit in the death of sportsmanship: sadly, coaches, parents, and our educational system are also offenders, and we'll explore each in the following pages.

By the time you're done reading this book, we hope you'll have achieved an understanding that stating the problem of poor sportsmanship, and pointing a finger at the culprits, is not enough. This dilemma requires a response, and our response must be to revive the morality of sports.

Sports are a metaphor for our lives. Consider that a game is essentially a series of choices influenced by each participant's actions and affecting everyone involved. In sports and in life, in whatever capacity we choose to participate, our behavior influences everyone watching, especially children. Our challenge is to help our children make wise choices, and we can begin to help them by encouraging positive decision-making by athletes and coaches during games and practice, in effect reviving the good of sports.

# Contents

# The Death of
## Sportsmanship

# Chapter One

# The Death of Sportsmanship

"What you see is what you get."

That saying came into vogue some thirty years ago. It even became the chorus for a rhythm and blues song. Twist it slightly and it unlocks a fundamental truth regarding the future of society: our children will emulate what they see—from their parents, teachers, and coaches, and, via the media, from their sports heroes.

What they see is what we will get.

In this book, you'll see the phrase "observational learning," an academic definition of "What our youth see is what our society will see in them."

It might sound like the fall of the Roman Empire, Armageddon, or some other cataclysm, but the argument has been made before that how a society plays its games is a reflection of its values, virtues, and problems. From any reasonable standpoint, sportsmanship, if not dead, is seriously ill. My goal is to help bring it back.

One of the most common human tendencies is to assign blame. To understand the demise of sportsmanship, the cause of death must be determined. That's the easy part. Rip the pages from magazines and newspapers; tape daily episodes of ESPN's SportsCenter; scan the Internet, and you'll be overloaded with all the evidence that any court would require.

My charge is to go beyond assigning blame. I'll explore the four fundamental factors that I assert are the main culprits in the death of sportsmanship. More important, I'll be solution-oriented.

To be so, a simple question must be asked: Am I desperately parading solutions around in search of a problem? I think not.

One might wonder: Why should any of us care? A better question: What is the case for sportsmanship? At its basic level, sportsmanship is human interaction in the context of athletic competition. One could find millions of sources on the human need for a sense of belonging. That urge is what drives many youths to sports; it's also what drives other youths to street gangs.

Is it that simple—play sports or join a gang? Certainly not. It is proven, though, that children will fill gaps in their lives. Our challenge is to help them make wise choices. Those of you who've ever participated in sports at any organized level surely heard one of your first coaches teach a basic lesson: sports are a metaphor for life. For the most part, we've believed that lesson. Our coaches' words have proven true—for good and bad. If only the good of sport could be preserved—what life lessons could be taught!

I approach this assertion from a variety of perspectives.

- *A former youth sports athlete;*

- *A walk-on who would become an All-SEC punter;*

- *A player who would be drafted by the NFL;*

- *A parent with children in youth-league sports;*

- *A person who has spent the past eight years studying the link between education, citizenship, and sports.*

Today, I'm no longer an athlete—not counting time in the gym or on the golf course. I'm just a fan.

My goal, without doubt, is ambitious: It is to help lay the foundation for a culture change that will ensure that sports remain an integral part of our nation's fabric. From my vantage point, I see sports dividing us more than uniting us. It's simply a reflection of society, which is more partisan than ever. Look at our nation's capital for example: democrats and republicans battle at a shrill pitch over nearly every issue.

My fear is that as the games take on greater intensity, more and more children will just opt to stay away, retreating to other, less healthy activities that do not offer the opportunity to build individual and team skills.

Many words have evolved over time. One of these is "sportsmanship." Today, I fear, the notion of sportsmanship connotes weakness. If one is a good sport, then one must not care whether one wins or loses. There's an oft-quoted saying: "Show me a good loser—and I'll show you a loser." That attitude is prevalent in sports, from the major leagues to the recreational leagues. Instead of a culture of healthy, friendly competition, we've seen the creation of a culture of haves and have-nots, winners and losers whose societal worth has been differentiated by the final numbers on a scoreboard. "Smack" and "trash talk" and similar phrases have become part of the everyday sports vocabulary.

My fundamental approach is the notion that sportsmanship must be taught as a basic skill, just like reading, writing, and arithmetic, and parents, teachers, and coaches must teach it. Unfortunately, my research shows that sportsmanship also must be taught to parents, teachers, and coaches. Odd as it may seem, it must be practiced by young athletes, just like free throws in the backyard and batting practice in the cage.

The assertions in this book are reinforced by research: first my own, then my company's, as well as that of respected leaders in education, athletics, and behavioral science. I don't seek to reinvent the wheel, but merely to re-inflate the tire.

The skills and strategies that I'll expound upon are simple and, more important, doable. Otherwise, sports will reach an important crossroads where the wrong path will lead to athletics being solely for the outstanding athletes. We are not all athletically gifted, but for those who love the game, there should be a role, particularly at the beginning levels. At that level of sport, the goals should be having fun, developing teamwork skills, and developing individual physical and mental skills.

I share these concerns because of my belief that for decades, the

American virtue of sportsmanship has been under attack, primarily from within. The attack has been launched in four areas. Assuredly, systemic changes must be made to those four areas, the four culprits in the death of sportsmanship.

**Role Models.** We'll view role models from two perspectives. In the next chapter, we'll look at the examples we see from our athletes, brought to us by the media. In a later chapter, we'll view the coach as a role model.

Decades ago, we knew our heroes from a distance: a baseball card, a friendly interview on the game of the week and the like. The 10,000-foot view we had years ago has been replaced by today's microscopic view, which has made it easier to see the warts. The average fan didn't know about the continual carousing of many star athletes of bygone days, but then, the athletes of decades past played without ESPN, talk radio, and the Internet.

The old school athlete often had an off-season job to pay the bills; only a few superstars could afford to live on the salaries their athletic feats earned. Major League Baseball entered the era of free agency by way of court order. With athletes in a better position to negotiate contracts, the big-money era of sports began. Major-league ballplayers who are leaders at their positions easily command salaries in excess of $10 million per season. The same is true of National Basketball Association stars.

The media has exploded in its coverage of sports. Thirty years ago, the phrase "Game of the Week" was prevalent. No national network was dedicated solely to sports. The Internet was a mere dream, and talk radio was confined to a few shows in the nation's largest media markets.

ESPN, the sports media conglomerate, bills itself as "The Worldwide Leader in Sports," and who's to argue? The major broadcast networks have their multimedia presence as well. The Internet provides sports on demand. Any city of any size surely has a sports talk radio show; usually, the most bombastic are the most popular.

As media exposure has grown, so has the insatiable desire of many athletes to be seen, creating the likes of "T.O.," Terrell Owens, troubled star of the National Football League, who has danced on the star logo at Texas Stadium, pulled a Sharpie from his sock to autograph the football he had just carried into the end zone for a touchdown, and other look-at-me hijinks. The media hasn't disappointed T.O. and those others who crave attention. Arguably the greatest moment in women's team sports was the 1999 FIFA World Cup. Think for a second about that event and what comes to mind: Brandi Chastain removing her shirt in celebration, and revealing her bra. That's what made it onto the cover of *Sports Illustrated*. Brandi has even written a book entitled *It's Not About The Bra*. Unfortunately, it's too late for that. Our children learned from Brandi's example — if not the first time they saw it live, then the hundreds of times they saw it on replay. Why?

Some may view the actions of Owens and others as mere harmless fun. That's not so for youth-league players and high school athletes and adults in recreational leagues. Athletes at all levels must be taught the effects of their acts on their opponents. Respect is a valued notion, but is often misunderstood. To respect the game requires respecting the opponent.

When a player celebrates an individual play, he or she probably hasn't considered the help they got to achieve that success. Consider the effort your opponent put into the game; think about what your teammate did with a pass or a block. John Donne told us, "No man is an island...." He was right.

One of the great difficulties is to effect change in the media. It must be done through the remote control, the switch of the radio dial, and the use of the Internet search engine. The lines between journalism and entertainment are continually blurred. We must strive to see clearly.

No one has a better chance to shape the athlete than the coach has. Parents impart a value system to a child, but we must be honest and acknowledge that peer pressure chips away at many children's values. In the context of a team sport, the coach is the law. What he or she asks for is generally what the player will provide.

Coaches, you can make a huge difference. Later, I'll introduce you to one who made a huge difference in my life.

**Society.** Don't be deceived: what we see on television is what we've asked to see. If society as a whole weren't interested in the latest brawl on the field, attention-grabbing celebration dances, and the like, they wouldn't be on TV, they would be mere blips on the Internet, and they wouldn't be talked about on the radio.

Of course, we know what has happened. We've asked for more. Why does ESPN have so many different channels? We watch them all. Why have steroids become prevalent? We demand physical perfection from our athletes. If an offensive lineman can max out his bench press at 500 pounds, then we want our team to have linemen who lift 550.

Perhaps it is here that the coach has contributed to the death of sportsmanship. Many have succumbed to the victory-at-any-price logic that society has pushed upon them. It has driven them to play ineligible players, use strategies that involve breaking the rules of the game, and employ questionable motivational and skill-building strategies. We've seen the negative transformation of the "whatever it takes" philosophy—a work-ethic-based notion that one should keep trying within acceptable boundaries of good behavior—into "by any means necessary."

Beginning geometry teaches the basic rule that the shortest distance between two points is a straight line. Sadly, society advances the idea that the shortest distance between two points is the shortcut.

One of the thoughts I'll advance is that steroid use is first and foremost a sportsmanship issue. Just as the team that uses ineligible players is guilty of poor sportsmanship, and just as the major leaguer who puts cork in his bat is guilty of poor sportsmanship, so is the steroid user. The added injurious effect is that the user jeopardizes his or her health. The mindset "It's cheating only if you get caught" permeates society. The truth is, if you cheat, you're cheating.

The battle of steroids won't be won by testing, but by education at the front end. I'll provide a glimpse at research that confirms the notion that testing after the fact is of little use compared to strategies based on stopping the potential user in advance.

**Education.** It's the job of our schools to not only teach reading, writing, and math, but also to help develop character. Some school systems do a better job of it than others do. The reality, though, is that because of government mandates such as "No Child Left Behind," schools are focused on testing results in mathematics and reading. Math and reading skills are no doubt critical to a child's future. They're part of the answer, but not the entire answer. In the body of one's future, math and reading are the muscles that strengthen the body. Character is the skeleton that holds it all together. And while schools are not the sole source—or even the primary source—of character education, they're a major component in teaching the common values of hard work, fair play, and human decency.

Thankfully, there are tools to help children of all ages learn to be better sports. Schools and educational athletics provide the best location for exposing young athletes to these tools. Today's youth appreciate interactive programs to develop skills in academics; instruction in sportsmanship skills can be delivered in similar fashion.

The partnership between education and athletics must be strong to help convey the need for sportsmanship. The potential for improvement is measurable. One additional link in the partnership is necessary to ensure success.

**Parents.** All parents want the best for their children, but sometimes we want too much. Perhaps, as many have argued, seeing our children on the field of play is akin to watching a home movie of our own youth, and we wish to relive a favorite memory or to rewrite history through the acts of our children.

Parents, as Dr. Shane Murphy writes, identify with their children. More important, Murphy writes of parental overidentification. The notion of overidentification pushes a parent over the line from supportive role model to negative influence.

We've seen extreme behavior in which parents have acted violently toward coaches, officials, players, and other parents. Their actions jeopardize the very future of the games they claim to love.

Simply put, parents are the first line of instruction and the best equipped to teach their children about sportsmanship through words, and more important, through their own deeds. All the encouragement received at home can be erased by an unseemly act in the stands at a game. How many of us have fallen prey to the heat of the moment?

Further, how many parents have clucked their tongues when someone questions a team's or a player's lack of sportsmanship? So often, parents will toss it aside, saying, "Kids will be kids" or, "It's what they see on TV."

Parents must understand their unique role in relation to their children's athletic endeavors. They are not the consultant, private coach, or critic. They should aim to be the fan, the encourager, and the number-one supporter. The parent must be the one whose goal is to make sure his child is having fun, developing teamwork skills, and developing his or her own skills as an athlete and as a person. Without the full partnership of parents, it won't work. Without parents, sportsmanship will not return.

Ultimately, we'll have a role to play in the resuscitation of sportsmanship, and we have a stake in its success. Sportsmanlike youth will grow into better leaders and better team players, and our nation will prosper for it.

For many, when memories start to fade, the times spent with teammates are the ones that endure, not necessarily the wins and losses. Without sportsmanship, the games could die and the memories would never be experienced.

The case for sportsmanship is simple: It's one of the easiest paths to satisfying that basic human need, the sense of belonging. Sportsmanship is inclusive. It breeds team and individual development and success. It celebrates the brotherhood of competition. It understands that there's value in defeat; that used properly, defeat can prepare you for future victory. Sportsmanship provides the foundation for nearly every social, professional, and family situation that one will encounter in a lifetime. Its return is crucial.

# The Death of Sportsmanship
## Causal Factors

### ROLE MODELS
**MEDIA HYPE**
➤ Rise of sports media
➤ 24/7 TV, radio, internet
➤ Pro athlete $$$ contracts

### SOCIETY
**WIN AT ALL COSTS**
➤ It's only cheating …
  If you get caught.

### EDUCATION
➤ NCLB FOCUS
➤ Reading & Math only
➤ Testing vs. Prevention

### PARENTS
**INCREASED INCIDENTS**
➤ Overidentification
➤ Ignoring the problem

## Chapter Two

# Role Models: The Message And the Messenger

On a September night in 1996, the umpire stared down the pitch that might or might not have grazed the outside edge of home plate. In a split second, he had to make the judgment call. With a flash of his right arm, John Hirschbeck called, "Strike three."

Roberto Alomar didn't like it one bit. After all, it wasn't like it was Greg Maddux or Roger Clemens on the mound. It was Paul Quantrill, a journeyman pitcher in every sense of the word. In the mind of an elite baseball player, the Paul Quantrills of the world didn't get this kind of call—certainly not against a perennial all-star like Alomar. It was a big game, even if it was the first inning. Alomar's Baltimore Orioles were fighting for an American League wild-card berth. One more win would clinch a spot in the playoffs.

To Alomar, every at-bat mattered, so he argued. Not surprisingly, Hirschbeck held firm. Alomar edged closer and said one of the magic words that results in a quick ejection. Baltimore manager Davey Johnson tried to intervene on Alomar's behalf, but it was too late. The ejection had come, and the harsh words continued.

Then, Roberto Alomar, a multiple winner of the Gold Glove for his stellar play at second base and a career .300 hitter with the Toronto Blue Jays, the Orioles, and later the Cleveland Indians, rewrote his legacy.

Alomar spit in Hirshbeck's face.

The images spilled out onto the airwaves for days. Sports editors and editorial-page editors condemned Alomar for his over-the-top reaction. The story even made it into a vice-presidential debate between Al Gore and Jack Kemp.

Major League Baseball, though, waffled about what to do with Alomar. Knowing that the players' union collective bargaining agreement allowed suspensions to be delayed until an appeals process was completed, Major League Baseball was stuck between a rock and a hard place. It first offered up a paltry five-game suspension, and braced for the appeal that was sure to come to keep Alomar playing through the playoffs. Alomar did appeal, effectively pushing his suspension into the 1997 season.

Although the two principals would ultimately reconcile and work together to raise money for a charity searching for a cure for the disease that killed Hirshbeck's son, a horrible seed had been planted.

Bitter fruit grew quickly. In 2002, the National Association of Sports Officials released a report entitled "Officials Under Attack 2002." It chronicled more than a dozen incidents in which players, coaches, and fans had assaulted officials. Within twenty-two days of the Alomar incident, NASO received the first three reports of like behavior in the amateur ranks. Pro athletes are role models, and the media is more than willing to show us their failings.

"Sports is just life with the volume turned up," Barry Mano says. "More and more people are interested in seeing the spotlight on them rather than the team. That has fed the problem."

The lesson is that role models matter. According to the old saying, life imitates art. In reality, life imitates life. What's seen on national television will be coming soon to a recreational-league or high school playing field near you. Count on it.

One of the greatest athletes to ever come from the area near my adopted hometown of Birmingham, Alabama, was my fellow Auburn University alumnus Charles Barkley.

Trouble seemed to follow Charles once he became professional. Occasionally, he looked for it. Charles, too, had a spitting episode, but he misfired, striking a young girl rather than the intended victim. He got in an altercation or two as well, once tossing an offending bar patron through a window.

11

Charles has always lived large. His opinions today are the cornerstone of TNT's coverage of the National Basketball Association. If Charles sees it or believes it, he'll speak out about it.

Despite our shared collegiate background, I disagree vehemently with something he said. At the height of his playing career in the early 1990s, Barkley was the focal point of a Nike TV advertisement. It provided him the forum to sidestep responsibility for his occasionally outrageous behavior.

> I am not paid to be a role model. I am paid to wreak havoc on a basketball court. Parents should be role models. Just because I can dunk a basketball, that doesn't mean I should raise your kid.

Like it or not, Charles—and all professional athletes—you are role models. Your every move with or without the ball, on or off the court, is mimicked to the smallest detail. Why do you think Nike, Under Armour, Gatorade, and many other corporations pay you millions to endorse their products? Because kids will watch, listen, and maybe most important, emulate what you do. You have to take the responsibility along with the wheelbarrow full of cash!

Seeing the smallest detail is ensured by the constant bombardment from the media culture we live in. ESPN has multiple channels showing highlight after highlight—many sending the wrong messages to impressionable young people. Talk radio and the Internet provide instant gratification to disaffected fans who are tired of higher ticket prices and escalating salaries.

More important, our children are seeing every image onscreen and are compelled to imitate. And it's not just in athletes. Last fall, researchers from Dartmouth Medical School attempted to determine how movies affect children's behavior. The researchers surveyed children ages ten to fourteen to see what they'd been watching. They determined that children with highest exposure to characters who smoked in movies were more than two and half times as likely to experiment with smoking themselves. Nearly 40 percent of the children who tried smoking acknowledged having done so because of the glamorization of smoking in movies.

"Because movie exposure to smoking is so pervasive, its impact on this age group outweighs whether peers or parents smoke or wherever the child is involved in other activities, like sports," said Dr. James Sargent, Dartmouth professor and lead author of the study.

Another study, released on August 8, 2006 by researchers at Wake Forest University School of Medicine in Winston-Salem, N.C., shows that the more an adolescent watched wrestling, the more likely he or she would be to engage in violence, such as physically or verbally abusive treatment of a date—called "date violence." The relationship between watching wrestling on TV and being the perpetrator of date violence was stronger among females.

Researchers asked a random sample of 2,238 North Carolina high school students how many times they had watched wrestling in the past two weeks. Among males, 24.6 percent had watched six or more times in those two weeks; among females, 9.1 percent had watched as heavily.

The researchers say adolescents who watch wrestling are exposed to a high frequency of violence between men and women, alcohol use, hearing women referred to as "bitch" or "ho," other verbal abuse, and physical abuse.

Lead author Robert H. DuRant, Ph.D., professor of pediatrics at Brenner Children's Hospital in Winston-Salem, expressed his concern regarding the "high level of violence that is portrayed on TV without any of the expected consequences occurring." He said this happens too often. "During one wrestling match a man dangled a woman upside down and then dropped her on her head, supposedly knocking her unconscious. In reality, I know this act would have probably broken her neck and killed her," he said.

While Dr. DuRant admits wrestling doesn't cause violence, he does say violence on TV can affect what's perceived as socially acceptable behavior. "If you don't like it, as a parent, call or write the FCC," said Dr. DuRant. "Talk to them or write to them. Let them know."

In layman's terms, the Dartmouth and Wake Forest studies confirm the simple idea that what our children see is what we will get from them. It happens in athletics as well. Dr. Albert Bandura is one of the leaders in the study of what's known as *observational learning*, or the social learning theory.

Observational learning, Bandura says, occurs when an observer changes his or her behavior to follow that of a role model. The consequences of a role model's behavior — whether through reinforcement or punishment — extend vicariously to the observer.

After reading more of Dr. Bandura's work, it became obvious why today's pro athletes have such an influence on our kids. As you look at the basic principles of the observational learning theory (below), think about how Alomar's incident, the media's discovery that Mark McGwire's home-run chase was aided by a supplement called *andro* (androstenedione), and the on-field antics of Terrell Owens and Brandi Chastain might be influencing our kids.

- *The more popular the potential role model, the more likely he or she is to be imitated.*

- *If the role model's behavior is rewarded with vast amounts of attention — particularly through the media — the more likely it is to be imitated.*

- *If the role model's behavior results in negative consequences, then the observer is less likely to imitate.*

- *A distinction is to be drawn between acquiring the behavior and performing. Oftentimes, observers see the behavior and exhibit much later when they see a motivation to do so.*

There are four separate components to observational learning processes: attention, retention, production and motivation.

Put simply, observers must pay attention to what's happening before them. They must have a reason to see the act. They must actively retain the information — such as the way the football player dunks the ball over the crossbar of the goalposts, or the way the basketball player maneuvers his body to dunk the ball. Production is the difficult part. As much as many want to, they can't dunk a basketball or turn back-flips. Ultimately, though, they must have motivation to do these acts. Usually, that incentive is to gather attention to him- or herself.

Bandura used a blow-up clown doll to test behaviors. The doll had a sand base that allowed it to pop back up after being struck. Prior to releasing a group of nursery-school children to play with the doll without supervision, all the children viewed videos of adults playing with the doll. As the adults kicked and struck the doll, some were praised for their strength, others were chastised and punished.

Predictably, the children's behavior modeled that of the adults. Those who saw adults praised for their behavior slugged and kicked at the clown doll; those who saw the group who were punished were less likely to lash out at it.

There has been disagreement as to what sex and violence on television have meant to our nation's children. Regarding violent images, some have argued that these images have created a false sense of fear of violence. Bandura says it does the opposite: violent images have helped create a spooky, violent new reality in America.

A study has shown that young men who ultimately committed violent acts were a little more likely to have experienced increased exposure to violent images during their youth. While the difference was only 10 percent, it's rightly said that when a program has millions of viewers, the number of new, potential victims grows.

So how does all of this relate to sports? In 1999, the US Women's Soccer Team won the FIFA World Cup—arguably the greatest moment in women's team sports. The final game was extremely dramatic, with a win for the US coming on Brandi Chastain's penalty kick. Over 90,000 people saw this tremendous victory in the stadium, and millions worldwide watched it on television. After scoring the winning goal, Brandi took off her shirt in celebration. The media discussed the "black bra incident" more than the game, drawing focus away from the incredible athletic team effort.

In 2000, Terrell Owens, a young wide receiver for the San Francisco 49ers, became a household name for his unusual celebration after scoring a pair of touchdowns against the Dallas Cowboys at

Texas Stadium. After his first touchdown, Owens sprinted fifty yards to mid-field and performed a celebratory dance on the blue star—the Cowboys' helmet logo—at the middle of the playing surface. The fans booed his antics vehemently. Later in the game, Owens scored again, dash to mid-field again, and repeated the dance. This time, George Teague, a Dallas safety, trailed Owens and, to the joy of the crowd, knocked him off the star. A mini-brawl ensued.

Owens, rightly or wrongly, had become a star—because of his dance on the Cowboys' symbol. He would ultimately be fined and suspended for a game—but that paled because of the perpetual bombardment of the images of his dance. And it would be far from the last time he would make the news.

Since the Dallas incident, Owens has, among other things:

- *Argued with an assistant coach on the sideline;*

- *Autographed a football following a touchdown, using a Sharpie he had hidden in his sock;*

- *Been suspended for conduct detrimental to his team.*

Owens has become the poster child for those who think some athletes are too focused on themselves and not enough on the team and the game. So, what does this type of behavior get you, besides a lot of media exposure? Well, contrary to what you might hear from NFL teams, it doesn't get you benched. Actually, it gets you a new $25 million deal with the Dallas Cowboys. If you're good you can get away with just about anything. Owens's confrontational style is being emulated all across the country. He was far from the first.

In the sensitive days when our nation is at war, using military metaphors has come under scrutiny. Former University of Miami star Kellen Winslow, Jr., found himself in the spotlight after calling himself a warrior following a game. And it's not only individuals. There have been incidents in which college football teams entering onto the field have run to the center prior to kickoff and danced or stomped on the opponents' logos. It's no surprise that many of these occurrences have led to shoving matches and hard feelings.

In a related activity, college football teams bring a school flag onto the field following a victory at their opponents' home fields. Team members wave the flag in front of their fans, and then drive it into the turf, a gesture signifying conquest of the land. The Southeastern Conference has banned the practice as a violation of its code of sportsmanship.

Many different behaviors confirm Bandura's study, as players and teams at all levels have committed acts that by any standard don't rise even to the most basic levels of sportsmanship. If sportsmanship is to be revived, images of positive role models must be discovered and highlighted, while negative role models must be confronted and encouraged to do better. If necessary, negative role models should be punished to the greatest possible extent.

Whether scientific or anecdotal, the evidence is clear that our children—and sometimes adults—are copying what they see on TV or read about on the Internet. Whether it's punching a clown doll or choreographing an end-zone dance, you can reasonably expect people to repeat the behavior. Science and history prove it to be so.

It happens in larger-scale events, too. The hooliganism that was limited to soccer-dominant countries in Europe and South America has found its way here with riotous celebrations after professional teams have won championships. The sustained riots in Detroit following the Tigers' 1984 World Series title proved that. Tragically, a young woman's life ended when the much-anticipated celebration of a Boston Red Sox World Series victory turned violent in 2004.

As violence begets violence, so does poor sportsmanship lead to more poor sportsmanship. It is my contention that steroid use, too, is an issue of sportsmanship. Among young athletes, it's escalating because of inability or unwillingness to tackle the issue. Just as young basketball players buy Nikes or some other brand of shoes because a favorite player wears them, so it goes with steroids and other banned substances.

With shoes, it goes back to Julius Erving and Magic Johnson sporting their Converse All-Stars; then there was Michael Jordan with his Nike Air Jordans, and so on. Remember the great home-run battle of 1998 between Mark McGwire and Sammy Sosa? The two traded bomb for bomb throughout the summer in pursuit of Roger Maris' previously unthinkable mark of sixty-one home runs in a season. Both blasted through that mark, and McGwire ended up with seventy—a record that would stand only until Barry Bonds hit seventy-three a few years later.

During the summer of '98, media reports surfaced that McGwire was using andro, a supplement not banned by baseball at the time, but banned by other sports. Available at nutrition stores, it was a powder to help build muscle. Once the stories hit, andro sales went through the roof, quadrupling in a short time. The new buyers were primarily teenage boys looking for a shortcut to bigger muscles.

The reports helped defuse whispers that McGwire might have been using something else, as he had bulked up considerably from the beginning of his career in the mid-1980s. Even so, McGwire's former teammate in Oakland, Jose Canseco, opined in his book, *Juiced,* that the bottle of andro stored in McGwire's locker was a smoke screen, and that he knew for certain that McGwire had used steroids. Before Congress, McGwire refused to specifically answer questions regarding steroids.

How do these things enter the minds of our youth? It's simple. In twenty-five years, ESPN has grown from a small, regional cable network to "The Worldwide Leader in Sports," as it calls itself. The major networks have always made sports available on television, but ESPN, which now has more than a half-dozen cable network offerings, has perfected the art.

ESPN's growth has launched careers of its announcers and commentators, and has added phrases to the sports vernacular—"Booyah!" and "You need a T.O., baby!" Regardless of who invented these phrases, ESPN pushed them into the national sports consciousness. Just as television has exploded in the past two and a half decades, so have talk radio and the Internet. People like Jim Rome and Colin Cowherd helped set the agenda for sports in the United States. Rome, based in California, calls his legions of listeners "clones," who are allowed to come "into the jungle" (on his show) and says that they must "have a take and it must not suck." Callers with viewpoints that Rome deems weak on facts or poorly delivered are cut off and ridiculed. Myriad Rome wannabes have popped up all over the nation.

With the advent of message boards, chat rooms, and blogs, everyone is now potentially an expert. This is partly rebellion against what some call the mainstream media (MSM). The other part is that there's finally an outlet for the ordinary person to have a say in the national discussion of sport. It's been two-edged: acts of poor sportsmanship are quickly ridiculed, but for others, such outlets are merely opportunities to be more outrageous than the previous speaker.

How do we change behavior? Reward those who have done well, for a start.

Rarely does a professional sport earn praise in this area, so I must offer thanks and praise for a few recent improvements.

NBA Commissioner David Stern showed the fortitude to require his league's players to lift their appearance to a higher standard, working with player's union leader Billy Hunter to institute a dress code for game day and travel.

Stern reacted forcefully when troubled star Ron Artest charged into the stands to confront a fan who had thrown beer on him. Artest received a fifty-game suspension for engaging the fan in a brawl.

NFL Commissioner Paul Tagliabue was quick to fine Terrel Owens, New Orleans Saints receiver Joe Horn, and others for over-the-top celebrations.

MLB Commissioner Bud Selig and union chief Don Fehr were slow to respond to the steroid scandal, but moved quickly on a plan once Congress got serious about intervention.

The NCAA (National Collegiate Athletic Association) has taken the heat, but instituted rules to limit celebrations on the field, both during and after games. While we can all point to a time when we wished that a penalty hadn't been called, I think we can safely say that we've prevented an escalation that would have embarrassed sport.

The Philadelphia Eagles deserve recognition for taking their best player off the field—not as much for his end-zone dances but for making disparaging remarks about his teammates.

All of this is good, but we need more. We need the leagues—the NHL included—to take a more proactive part in sportsmanship programs and agenda setting to help resuscitate sportsmanship. It's the age-old idea made popular in the 1970s TV commercial: Pay me now or pay me later. Giving our youth positive role models—such as David Robinson, Peyton Manning, and the like—helps build better citizens than does glorifying those who seek to elevate themselves at the expense of others. Working on the front end of any situation helps prevent problems later.

Role models, whether seen live or merely as momentary images on a TV screen, influence, for good or ill, the behavior of other athletes of all ages, from the eight-year-old Little Leaguer to the forty-five-year-old recreation-league player trying to recapture past glory.

While it may seem pie-in-the-sky, leaders of the professional and collegiate leagues have the best opportunity to effect change through their relationships with the media. If they agree that the highlight packages should be about the games and not about the celebrations and taunting, then they, the league leaders, can change it immediately. Enforce stiffer fines and you'll see the shameful behaviors end. I'm not naive enough to think it will all stop; in fact, I don't want all of it to stop. The first time I watched an NFL Films show about Dick Butkus and Deacon Jones, it was one of the most exciting things I'd ever seen. I've watched them all and continue to enjoy seeing the "other side" of the NFL. But those "old-school" guys had a different message and a different delivery. It wasn't about them, but about the team.

Undoubtedly, our children are looking for role models to emulate, and they'll find them somewhere. Will they find them spitting in an opponent's face, or extending a hand to help that same opponent off the ground?

The notions of responsibility, accountability, and consequences must be fostered at every level of every sport. The media can no longer hide behind the argument "Don't blame the messenger." The messenger isn't solely to blame, but the media can't deny that it could help change the agenda in the United States.

If sportsmanship is to be revived, then Charles Barkley must be declared wrong. Don't show me the money. Show me the great catches, the thundering dunks, and the long home runs.

And every now and then, show me the handshakes.

# Chapter Three

## Society: Instant Gratification's Bitter Fruit

Hardly a day passes without our hearing the beep or the ding—the chime that signals the end of the cooking (or re-heating cycle) of a microwave oven. The microwave may be the poster child of the instant gratification society we live in today. Or is it a cell phone, or maybe a TIVO? It's not enough to record events for posterity on a VCR or DVD recorder. We want to be able to rewind and watch the play again—even while the machine records what's happening in real time.

Society has never had more access. Early cell phones were in large bags for use in cars. Now we have Blue Tooth and Blackberries affording us instant mobile communication. I can't complain too loudly: these tools, along with the Internet, allow greater productivity in my work, and provide me easier access to my family when I'm traveling. Translated, I grumble about them, but I wouldn't do without them.

When the Internet came along, we didn't know what we had. We were in the infancy of becoming a computer-savvy society. We first learned of the immense research potential of the World Wide Web, and soon found how we could become the "global village" Marshall McLuhan wrote about decades ago.

Then, there's talk radio, which exploded at about the same time as the Internet. In many ways, the two are runaway trains on parallel tracks. In a nation founded on the bedrock of free speech, the ability to speak free is cheaper than ever.

With the Internet, the rage is now the "blog," vernacular for "Web log." We can all be commentators. With a few bucks and a little imagination, we can have our own Web page and pontificate on any issue. Our opinions can be tossed into the national discussion on any subject. We Americans, particularly our youth, are doubtless more technologically savvy than ever before. But it has come at a price.

Remember those cell phones that we've given to our children. Originally, cell phones went with traveling businessmen and women, then found their way to soccer moms who spent a good deal of time shuttling kids around town in the minivan.

Now, they're in the hands of children who lack the maturity to deal with the speed of today's society. Once, parents had to make sure their children didn't spend too much time on conventional telephones. Then parents had to worry about what Internet sites their children visited, and that advanced to what was being e-mailed back and forth. Now, the need for speed has led to instant messaging. And predators have found ways at every point to jump into the process.

What has this to do with sportsmanship? More than you might imagine. Instant gratification in communications and entertainment has spilled into our behavior in the sporting world. We've already discussed how the mainstream media has brought us closer to the games — for better or for worse.

Talk radio and message boards have helped foster a "win now" attitude that has boiled over on the airwaves and on the Internet. A fan can go to the game, then offer immediate feedback on the team's performance on a call-in show after the game, or post his thoughts on a message board as soon as a computer is handy.

The responses swing to extremes. Wins are viewed as the greatest occurrence since the discovery of polio vaccine. Losses are compared to the Hindenburg disaster. The coach who was the second coming of Vince Lombardi and John Wooden one day is an imbecile the next week. Players are called out for mistakes, and not just professional athletes; so are collegiate athletes and even those at the high school level. For the fan in the fortieth row, the more bombastic his opinions on the talk show or the message board, the more he becomes a celebrity himself. Chances are, your local sports talk show has regular callers who are known to the audience for their frequent calls and over-the-top views.

This filters down to children. Recall Bandura's research as mentioned in Chapter 2. What the children see on television, they are likely to repeat. In addition to what they see on the field, they can see poor behavior from fans on television and in person if they attend games.

Where poor sportsmanship is tolerated, you can expect to see more of it. The old joke about Santa Claus being booed by Philadelphia Eagles fans has reinforced a level of behavior in that city given the Greek name for—of all things—*brotherly love.*

A horrible tradition has emerged in cities that have won championships. When the Detroit Tigers won the World Series in 1984, the city burned with riots as if there were political unrest. The hordes in Boston went so wild after the Red Sox finally won the World Series that one woman died—struck in the eye by a policeman's rubber bullet—when police intervened to calm down the celebration.

What's the next generation to do? More than likely, without a culture change, it will do what ours did: up the ante, push the stakes a little higher, lower the standards a little more, and cause more problems for those who seek a return to civility in sport.

After all, talking trash isn't limited to the field of play. It's practiced in the stands, on the message boards, and on the airwaves of talk radio, and even in the workplace. How many of you have dreaded a Monday morning at the office, knowing that your team lost to its rival and a gloating coworker was lying in wait for you?

I have to be careful when making suggestions in this area: I have the disadvantage of having played college football and was fortunate enough to have been drafted by the Green Bay Packers. Disadvantage? Yes, in the sense that it would be easy for me to be arrogant regarding some of the voices talking about the games. It'd be easy to say that someone has no right to talk "because he never played the game, so he doesn't know what he's talking about."

Often, in fact, they *don't* know what they're talking about. But I must admit that, because of the availability of information—more games on TV, more technology to illustrate finer points of the game, and the like—more and more people do know some of what they're talking about. Now, everyone is a coach, so to speak.

Bandura didn't mention the evolution of video games in his research, but it's instructive concerning the evolution of our desire for immediate satisfaction. We started with "Pong"—beeps and boops that mimicked a game of Ping-Pong, and have evolved into highly intense games with near-virtual graphics.

Even as the NCAA has adopted rules to combat poor sportsmanship on the field, it has sanctioned, through its PlayStation2 game, players who score touchdowns dunking the ball over the upright in celebration. In another tip of the hat to reality, if a person sets up a "season" in the NCAA football game, players may be "suspended" for rule violations and other offenses. The more any facet of a video game makes it like the real thing, the more popular the game becomes.

In a game patterned on the NFL, injured players could get an injection on the sideline and reenter the fray. I applaud the NFL for pulling the license so their teams and players won't be portrayed this way in the future.

The intense desire to be just like the pros is driving the development of video games, and it's driving the development of youth-league sports, too.

Whatever the reason, there's little doubt that the men and women who officiate our children's games overwhelmingly believe that sportsmanship is the number-one problem in sports. In 2004, 550 sports officials were polled, and they pointed to four reasons for the lack of sportsmanship:

- *Professional athletes serving as poor role models;*

- *Parents allowing their children to act up, thinking it's part of the game;*

- *Coaches focused too heavily on winning;*

- *People in general lacking civility toward each other.*

I couldn't agree more. The first three are obviously narrow in scope, but the fourth, regarding society, is decidedly true.

It's not enough anymore for a basketball player to score a basket. He must dunk it if he can. It's not enough for a player to make a spectacular catch for a much-needed first down to keep a drive alive; he then has to get up and give a knee-bending first-down signal, á la Michael Irvin.

There was a time when scoring a basket, catching a big pass, or hitting a home run was enough, but, sadly for society, that time has gone. A rim-rattling dunk is expected, and a celebratory dance or scornful word for an opponent is even better. Not to do so displays weakness, and today's society doesn't tolerate weakness.

Is it that we're more attuned to athletes today? I don't think so. My generation and the one prior collected baseball cards. I had childhood friends who, when they played baseball, would loop their bats like Willie Stargell or even pop their elbows against their sides like Joe Morgan.

But in this video-driven generation, we see more than idiosyncrasies in batting stances. We have zoom lenses into the lives of athletes. We see their tattoos, and their warts—both literal and figurative. What's important about tattoos? The tattooed messages tell us what's important to the athlete—and society responds. On some athletes, it's a salute to family or faith; on others, it's a statement of independence, which is fine, but when the tattoo becomes more of a focus than the game, we have a problem.

Dr. Shane Murphy, author of *The Cheers and the Tears*, quotes sports sociologist Jay Coakley regarding how sports, particularly emerging sports, gain wider appeal: greater danger, greater attention. This spreads the win-at-all-costs mentality so prevalent today.

In 1978, in a laudable progressive step, the Michigan Legislature created the Institute for the Study of Youth and Sport, whose main mission was to study the good and the bad in youth sports and produce materials to improve the quality of behavior.

The institute shared a study regarding the behavior of two groups of young boys. One group's physical education class participated in the "Kickball World Series," while the other was turned loose for free play. The result? Those competing in the so-called World Series exhibited worse behavior than those engaged in free play.

The obvious conclusion is an important message: there can be too much too soon for youth in sports. Children now win "state championships" long before they reach high school age. Boys and girls who have yet to reach junior high are now playing on traveling baseball teams. Single-sport specialization is prevalent as baseball teams spend their autumns on the road rather than playing football or other fall sports.

This type of specialization resulted in the widely known dismissal of a successful basketball coach from an Alabama high school. The coach, one year removed from a state championship, was fired for telling his players that if they wanted to play basketball they had to give up other sports. The coach didn't argue. He told reporters that the principal's objection was true—he wanted his players to be basketball players only. The principal held the wider view, seeing basketball as a seasonal sport.

My view aligns with the principal's; I believe that kids shouldn't be forced to choose a single sport. If a child wants to play football and baseball and can handle his or her academics, then so be it. Part of the joy of the high school experience is its variety and the friends you make along the way. Pigeonholing students into one area diminishes that.

Each weekend, ABC's Wide World of Sports brought us "the human drama of sport...the thrill of victory...the agony of defeat." Every sports fan of a certain age can still remember the sight of the ski jumper tumbling off the ramp. It's the experience that those of us who've passed the age of playing the game now seek—the human drama.

Murphy acknowledges this. "We enjoy learning about the players and hearing their stories and we identify with many of the players in some way (ethnicity, location, background, lost a father, cut from high school team, etc.). This human element has increased the mass audience viewing...." Murphy insists that we're looking for a repeat performance.

By his logic, NCAA basketball fans are looking for the next North Carolina State and Villanova. Baseball fans are looking for the next Mark McGwire and Sammy Sosa battle. Golf fans are looking for the next John Daly—a real-life Cinderella out of nowhere who won the PGA Championship.

Remember this lesson: in society's mind, bigger is better. When I arrived at Auburn University as a walk-on punter, Jordan-Hare Stadium seated 72,000. It expanded to 87,000-plus in 1987. People wonder when it will expand again. The same goes for the first university I attended, the University of Tennessee. Neyland Stadium now seats well over 100,000.

But bigger isn't always better with athletes. Steroids have been having an effect on sport for nearly three decades. We've seen the negative effects they've had on athletes whose bodies have turned on them. As he lay dying, Lyle Alzado, the former Denver Bronco and Oakland Raider, revealed that using steroids had snuffed out his life. His disclosure helped focus the spotlight on an embarrassment to the NFL.

Society's reaction can make a difference. The best example is Major League Baseball's response to the steroid issue. Left to their own devices, the owners and the players' union were in no hurry to take any substantive steps.

In 2005, Congress, led by Senator John McCain, decided to throw baseball a proverbial high and tight fastball, calling a string of players and officials before committees, and leaving Mark McGwire to stumble and bumble through his testimony. It wasn't what McGwire said, but rather what he wouldn't say.

Suddenly, Commissioner Bud Selig and union chief Don Fehr were in the mood to solve a problem. The result was a stricter testing and penalty program. And the testimony continued. Baltimore Oriole standout Rafael Palmeiro took a different approach: he vehemently denied ever using steroids and even had the guts (or stupidity) to point his finger at the distinguished panel.

Palmeiro's words came back to bite him when he tested positive for steroids later in the season. Ultimately, he was suspended for ten games as a first-time offender, but he's become radioactive to the Orioles and other teams. It's questionable whether he'll play again, despite his claims that he never intentionally took steroids.

Finally, Major League Baseball put teeth in its steroid policy. Why? Because of public outrage. Congress takes its cue from the people, and acted because the public made it clear that they'd seen enough regarding steroids. Let's be thankful for that.

So, what have steroids to do with sportsmanship? Let's think through the issues and some suggested solutions. A major issue today is that young athletes are doing steroids.

The CDC reported that steroid use among high school students more than doubled from 1991 to 2003. National surveys indicate 3–3.5 percent of high school students have used steroids.

Posted 5/4/2005
**"School tackles alarming subject: Steroid use"**
by David Leon Moore, *USA Today*

In 2003, Centers for Disease Control's Youth Risk Behavior Surveillance System found that 6.1 percent of respondents reported having taken a steroid injection or pill without a doctor's prescription at least once. Last year, the University of Michigan's Monitoring the Future survey found that 3.4 percent of high school seniors said they had taken steroids.

**"Prep Programs Debate Merits of Steroid Testing"**
by Josh Barr, *Washington Post* Staff Writer, Thursday, May 26, 2005, D01.

Keep in mind that those numbers, while alarming, pale in comparison to the percentage of teens who use alcohol, marijuana, X, methamphetamine ("meth"), and other illicit drugs. In discussions throughout the country, we've seen numbers suggesting that steroids are perhaps twelfth on the list of illicit drugs teens are using. But because our professional sports heroes might have used steroids, which may cause the records they hold to be marked with asterisks, many legislators have chosen to make steroids a major issue. Steroid use is indeed a major issue, but is it more important than alcohol, tobacco, or other recreational drug use by teens? Of course not. Part of the reason why steroid use receives so much attention at every level is... *it's cheating!* That is a sportsmanship issue.

My travels and our company's business relationships have given me the opportunity to meet some of the most influential leaders in K-12 educational athletics. Their experience is invaluable, as is their perspective on dealing with a variety of issues related to school athletics. One such group is the University Interscholastic League (UIL) in Texas. Dr. Bill Farney, Executive Director, and Dr. Charles Briethaupt, Assistant Director, are charged with running junior and high school extracurricular activities. All of America knows how big high school football is in Texas. Imagine all the issues the UIL staff and their twenty-eight-member legislative council face. A few years ago they were confronted with several student-athletes who were using steroids.

Dr. Charles Briethaupt, on the influence of the professional athlete:

> The media circus surrounding Barry Bonds and other pro athletes who have allegedly used steroids has created interest among high school athletes. The more it is discussed in negative tones, the more interest is piqued among students. When they read or hear that athletes can make great gains in strength and speed, many are influenced to consider taking risks as well. The more attention these athletes receive, the more interested our young athletes are in taking a chance.

So how does Dr. Briethaupt see the UIL best dealing with this issue?

> State associations like the UIL must do what they do best, and that is to educate. While many call for us to test, we believe it is more important to teach kids how to make quality decisions that will impact them for a lifetime. Our number-one issue today is communicating

30

the negative impact of steroid abuse to all concerned. The education of students is only one arena. We must reach parents and coaches in order to effectively impact students. [Of all the parties involved, experts agree that parents are the key to stopping the use and abuse.] Parents are a key ingredient to any positive steroid-education program. It takes well-informed parents to be able to monitor the actions of our youth today.

So how can the public effect change in the world of athletics? Get involved. Use your voice to encourage our young athletes — at the games, on talk radio, on message boards, and anywhere else that you can be heard.

Apply positive pressure on youth leagues you're involved in to make sportsmanship a true priority. Create the expectation of sportsmanship rather than trash-talking and inappropriate play. Emphasize the dangers of steroids.

Whether you realize it or not, it was your outrage that helped make baseball take a stand against steroids. It will take similar societal outrage to stop the culture of trash-talking, cheating, and show boating. Don't run from talk radio. Make a call. Be heard. Don't hit the red "X" in the upper-right corner of the online message board. Make your positive opinion known. We don't have to continue chasing the bigger, the stronger, and the faster. We have enough to enjoy in sports — if we don't ruin it by trying to continue make it bigger, stronger, and faster.

Resist the temptation to try to make youth sports more than what they were intended to be: an opportunity to grow and learn. Resist the temptation to be the team's number-one critic. Realize that the child in the stands next to you — whether it's your child or someone else's — hears every word you say and is likely to repeat it. History, we know, repeats itself.

So let's make history the right way.

## Chapter Four

# Parents:
# Teach Your Children Well

The issue of sportsmanship, the lack of it and the impending death of it, became crystal clear in my role as a parent. A few years ago, when helping kids develop academic skills was the major thrust of my life's work, I was at a youth soccer game. There was nothing special about that Saturday morning—except that it changed my life forever.

Prior to the game, a player on one of the teams was yelling at a player on an opposing team. The shouting was actually smack-talking. What made it even worse was these kids were seven years old! I was flabbergasted.

By no means am I a sheltered person. Remember, I played college football; my final game was the Sugar Bowl against the Florida State Seminoles, and Deion Sanders was the nation's leading punt returner. Deion knew how to talk. Still does. I didn't expect a seven-year-old girl to start rattling off what her team was going to do to their opponents. Two things popped into my head. This girl has a coach; what's this coach teaching these kids? More important, this girl is somebody's daughter.

From that point on, the noise in the stands at every game I've attended has become more than background noise. Sadly, it's often a painful reminder of why sportsmanship is in so much trouble today. Mom and Dad, we've been willing participants in the creation of a culture that tolerates bad sportsmanship, and furthermore we've been a major part of the problem.

Through my travels and our company's extensive research into this problem since 2000, it still amazes me that every parent, teacher, and coach I've met abhors the problem and can tell me a story about it, but I've yet to meet a single person who recognizes that he or she *is* the problem. All parents think it's someone else, and, based on our research, you're probably as guilty as the next one. I found out that I was.

We've all seen the wild stories in the news. In 2000, a Massachusetts man beat his son's hockey coach to death at the team's practice, leading to a manslaughter conviction.

And last summer, we were surely all stunned when a man who'd been banned from the practice field and games walked into a Texas high school football coach's office and shot the coach.

No reasonable person would say these events have contributed to sport, or are just "part of the game."

The problem involving you and me as parents of young athletes is far more subtle than that.

Numerous books and hours of research in the field of behavioral psychology point to the fact that a child's view of self is determined more by what he hears than by looking at himself in the mirror.

There are countless examples of kids quitting sports, or worse, still playing them but hating it because of the "coaching from the stands," the criticism, the critiquing after a game, and the tremendous pressure their own parents place on kids. In one discussion I had, a young girl explained how she dreaded the drive home from tennis matches because of the discussions with her father. I asked her if it was better when she won. She said, "Not really, because there's always something to critique." She ended up hating tennis, dreaded spending time with her dad, and looks back on that part of her childhood as being miserable. She was twelve. How sad. She said to me, "I know my dad loves me, but I wish he would have just backed off and let me enjoy being a kid and playing tennis. I knew I wouldn't be Chris Everett, but he kept thinking I might."

If faultfinding words spoken during the car ride home hurt, then how much deeper do the words cut when shouted from the stands?

Do parents understand that when they yell for their son or daughter to do something specific on the field of play—"Shoot the ball!" or "Go to third base!"—that they could be telling their child to do precisely the opposite of what the coach has said to do? Do you have any idea what goes through your kid's brain when she hears you tell her something that, to you, is simple, positive, and obvious, like "Choke up on the bat"? Well, I didn't, and I think it'll shock you as well.

As our behavioral psychologists came back with their findings on how best to impact parental behavior at ball games, they told us a story. Based on all the research and interviews with players, parents, and coaches, they said that when a parent yells anything specific from the stands, it often makes the child nervous and stressed. When you say something like "Hey, Matt, choke up on the bat!" your child becomes very aware of the stage he is now on. This immediately creates pressure to do well, to please you, to perform, and makes the child focus entirely on the outcome of that play. I don't think that's what parents are trying to do. I know that I wasn't.

When this information came back to me, it immediately registered with me regarding my son and Little League baseball. I went home that night and asked my son about it. I could tell he didn't want to hurt my feelings, which confirmed my suspicion. He finally admitted that when he hears my voice as he's getting up the plate, it makes him nervous. Wow! I hugged him, told him how sorry I was, and swore I'd never do it again. I'm the guy trying to help fix all of this, and here I am making Little League ball *not fun* for my son. A very humbling experience. Stop for a minute and think about how you behave at your children or grandchildren's games.

Coaching should be left to the team's coach, to whom we parents have *entrusted* our children, so, as that word suggests, trust the coach!

In his book *Raising a Good Sport in an In-Your-Face World,* Dr. George Selleck had the best idea about dealing with your child in the realm of sport.

"Never compare your children to anyone else. They will do enough of this on their own. Your job is to help your children recognize their individual worth and the things that make them unique."

Dr. Selleck is absolutely right. I know from firsthand experience. My father, Stan Shulman, was phenomenal in helping me understand my individual worth. Because I was human, I still compared myself to others. All children do. Don't make it easier for them to do so by heaping it on.

The thing that bothered me during my youth as I sought the goal of playing football in college and in the NFL was my lack of height. No amount of work could change that. I looked at all the great punters, and most of them were tall. During our college days, some friends and I went to the Atlanta suburbs to watch the Falcons scrimmage against the Miami Dolphins in training camp.

I had the opportunity to watch one of the greatest punters of all time. Reggie Roby, who passed away last year, was an All-American at the University of Iowa and a perennial All-Pro with the Dolphins. Reggie looked more like an offensive tackle than a punter, and the sound when his foot hit the ball was like a gunshot.

I wanted to kick like Reggie Roby, but for me to kick the best Brian Shulman could kick would take my own hard work. I could lift weights, run, practice my technique, and develop mental toughness, but none of it would make me any taller. In golfer's jargon, my legs were 7-irons, not 3-irons.

All along the way, my parents encouraged me to be the best Brian I could be. I might not have appreciated it enough then, but I certainly do now. I can't imagine what I'd be like mentally and emotionally had they tied my self-worth to my play on the field. I hurt for those kids with parents who are like that, parents who make sports awful for them.

Earlier, I introduced the idea of overidentification. The best expert I know of on this subject is Dr. Shane Murphy, who wrote *The Cheers and the Tears*. He outlines a progression that takes the parent from one who loves and wishes the best for the child to one who becomes a monster.

Murphy writes that all parents love their children and want to see them do well, but the progression can get out of control. The parents' overidentification often becomes less about their children having fun and more about the parents' self-worth and reliving their own past triumphs or trying to succeed vicariously through their child to compensate for their own youthful failures.

Wait a minute! My self-worth as a parent is tied to how well my son does on the field or how well my daughter does on the tennis court? Very scary, very powerful, and sadly for many kids today, very true. Remember Todd Marinovich? Perhaps the poster child for an over-identifying parent. The child-phenom southpaw quarterback was never allowed to have any junk food or soft drinks. Never! Well... until he got to USC, that is. Then things moved quickly from junk food to illicit drugs and a troubled off-field life that ultimately ruined his pro football career. So how do parents become so misguided? Here's how Dr. Murphy outlines the progression:

- *I love my child.*

- *I want him or her to be happy.*

- *I know my kid tries hard in practice and games.*

- *I know I've made sacrifices in time and money for them to be able to play.*

- *I know I could have been better if I had been pushed and told what to do.*

- *My kid deserves to be successful in athletics, and I want it for him or her.*

- *I want my child to be better than that other parent's child.*

- *I want to be better than that other parent is, and I can be if my child is successful.*

- *It's my job to make sure that my child fulfills our goals and dreams—regardless of whether they're truly his or hers.*

This behavior manifests itself during games. Jon Hellstedt, a leading sports psychologist, makes a point that reinforces Murphy's argument. Parents' greatest strengths—unwavering support for their children and willingness to make sacrifices for their children's advancement—combine to form their greatest weakness.

What we must understand is that there's a fine line between encouragement and over-involvement in our children's games.

Positive parents encourage their children no matter the outcome of any play or the final score of any game. They carpool their children to practice, buy whatever equipment their children need (within reason), and help the kids practice at home if the kids want to.

The negative parent coaches from the stands, often disagreeing with what the team's coach has instructed. The bottom line is, not every play is designed for your child to shoot the basketball. Sometimes, the risk isn't worth the potential reward of trying to run to third base. Maybe the coach wants the batter coming up after your child to bat with runners on base, rather than leading off the next inning after your Bobby or Mary was thrown out at third to end this one. Leave the strategy to the coaches.

The fact that what our children see is what we'll get from them in the future applies especially to parents. How you react to situations in life will shape the way your child reacts to similar situations in his or her future.

If you display inappropriate behavior, how do you think your children will behave later on? One expression common today is fans' anger about high ticket prices. "I paid $75 for this ticket, so I'll say what I darn well want to!" That attitude is questionable at best, but no one can argue that it doesn't belong at the Little League field or in the stands at a high school game.

How does it happen in the first place? The parent probably has low self-esteem and often takes his or her child's performance in athletics personally. This manifests in complaining about the child's performance and berating officials and coaches.

Few parents will acknowledge that they're the ones who yell at their children too much or berate coaches and officials. It takes honest introspection to evaluate how each of us behaves. In my interview with him, Dr. Murphy offered a great suggestion as to how to better manage these issues. Each league should form a parents' committee that's focused exclusively on sportsmanship in the stands. Each team should then have a couple of parents form a team committee. These committees should focus on behavior among parents in the stands and address the issues immediately with their own teams. What an obvious yet regrettably underused idea! And it's not just about managing sportsmanship behavior toward your own kids or the opposing teams. Officials and coaches are often the targets of parents' abuse. In youth leagues, coaches are volunteers, and officials receive nominal pay.

Randal Beesley, who has officiated football games involving players from first grade all the way up to the NFL, observes that parental behavior is the same regardless of the level of competition. "Parents are so emotionally tied to the games," he says. "In youth leagues, they should be emotionally tied to the learning experience for their children.

"I've heard the same things over and over again: we're cheating, we don't know the rules, and every obscenity in the world. And this has come at youth league games, junior high games, and high school games."

Beesley knows what it's like to be chased by angry parents and to be escorted out of town by police officers.

"It's hard to believe," he said, "but it's true."

To rebuild the core of sportsmanship, parents must take a major role in making it happen. You must keep your children's goals at the forefront and never stray from them. Understand what your child wants from playing sports—more than likely, it's just a way to have fun.

Just as important, parents, be a role model, not only for your children, but also for other parents.

How do you do that? Here's a list for starters. Some of it may seem entirely contrary to human nature:

- Compliment the other team by telling the parents how well their kids played.

- Before you offer criticism to your child (hopefully constructive in nature), make sure that what you're going to say is absolutely crucial to your child's success. Ask yourself whether it could wait a week or a month to see if the child learns it on his or her own. If you still need to say it, then make sure you say something positive to your child first.

- Never try to coach your child during a game or practice.

- Compliment the officials.

That last one is a challenge to all parents. It surely is for me, because I'm used to a coach with intensity. My college football coach, Pat Dye, is one of the most intense people I've ever known. But Coach Dye was coaching college players, not second graders who want to watch the Disney Channel when they get home.

For youth leagues, particular for elementary school students, it's imperative to educate parents about the purpose of the league and to identify the best people to coach. Finding the right coaches for children who are just beginning to play the game is vital. The goals for youth sports should be: 1) to teach the rules and the skills of game; 2) to help identify whether a child has a love for the game; and 3) to build teamwork skills.

Winning and losing should be of minimal concern. Teaching your child how to win and lose with grace is paramount. Undoubtedly, winning is fun, but it's temporary. Teams might go undefeated for a season, but at some point, we all suffer loss—on the job, losing a loved one, or other experience.

As parents, our job is to shepherd our children, not live vicariously through them.

Instead of asking your child, "Did you win?" ask, "Did you have fun?"

Unsportsmanlike behavior is nothing new. Back in the early days of Little League Baseball, prior to World War II, there was a practice that has value today. Unruly parents were given a handwritten note that simply stated, "The game is for the children. Please leave them alone so they can play the game."

The name of the national baseball league, the PONY League, was an acronym of "Protect Our Neighborhood Youth." Who knew that we'd need to protect them from their parents and coaches?

Make no mistake: our children, particularly those ages eight to fourteen, are desperately seeking role models. Someone *will* show them how to act, parents, and it had better be you. It's your job to teach your child how to shake someone's hand; to teach your child how to be a team player; to teach your child that there's something greater than the individual. These are learned behaviors, and they need teachers.

Here's what we can do now to help parents practice better sportsmanship, and in turn help their children practice better sportsmanship.

**Communication.** It will take continued communication between parents, coaches, school administrators, and league administrators.

**Let the kids talk.** Children should feel empowered to tell their parents to chill out. Kids, tell your parents how you feel and what you want from them. Parents, don't let positive values be compromised, but be prepared to make positive changes.

**A new culture.** Set high expectations for parental behavior.

**Leave the officials alone.** Understand why officials are there in the first place. Realize that officials are people just like you. They're trying to do a good job. They don't do it for the money. Yelling at them doesn't help.

It doesn't take a village to raise a child to be a good sport. It takes parents and coaches working together.

## Chapter Five

# Our Schools: Leaving Sportsmanship Behind?

There are countless theories on where our schools went wrong: lack of central control; not enough local control. Too much emphasis on math and science; not enough technology, math, and science. Lack of parental involvement. Lack of prayer in schools; fixation on issues like prayer in schools. Teachers' unions; low pay for teachers.

Upon assuming the presidency, George W. Bush outlined a program that he believed would help restore the American education system. "No Child Left Behind" was the idea.

"These reforms express my deep belief in our public schools and their mission to build the mind and character of every child, from every background, in every part of America." President Bush said in January 2001, just days into his term.

A year later, he was signing the landmark legislation into law. Has it worked? It depends on whom you ask. It has put emphasis on accountability and focused on reading and mathematics. With only so much time in the day and an emphasis on math and reading, something has to take a back seat. It only takes a few court decisions against a teacher or coach for disciplining a student or student-athlete for the rest of the K–12 educators and coaches to back off from disciplining children for poor behavior. All this creates an environment that doesn't emphasize character education.

Dr. Clem Mejia, Regional Superintendent, Kane County Regional Office of Education, has a unique perspective on this issue. The former teacher and junior high school coach in football, basketball, and track is now superintendent of education. Dr. Mejia is first a father of two, one a senior football player and three-time all-conference wrestler whom he coached in soccer years ago. In Dr. Mejia's role as regional superintendent, he is responsible for 175 schools in Kane County, one of the collar counties of Chicago. A veteran of more than thirty-five years in the industry, Dr. Mejia is charged with educating the "whole" child, not just children's academic well-being.

> I've seen a dramatic change in the past few years. When my son was playing youth soccer there wasn't nearly the emphasis on winning that there is today. We have to constantly remind our parents and coaches that our goal is to have fun and teach life lessons more than win state championships. I'm not sure why, but many folks seem to think that if you are a good sport then you must not be a winner. When I was growing up that just wasn't the case.

So how does Dr. Mejia view the proper role of the teacher in this process?

> Sports provide a great opportunity to reveal the character of a person. All of our students go to physical education and many participate in school sports or outside club programs. We have many opportunities to teach during that time and then subsequently back in the classroom. The proper attitude must be modeled early. Due to the strong influence of professional athletes and the nonstop media coverage of some of these athletes' negative behavior, it was critical to address this issue with our students. We needed to formalize our teaching of sportsmanship to combat all of these negative influences. We were surprised at just how little our students knew about sportsmanship, and at the impact that lack of knowledge was having on our classroom behavior and academic teaching experience.

I was curious as to how Dr. Mejia deals with parents and their influence in this area.

Parents have the greatest influence on this issue, but several years ago we started seeing that parents were actually becoming major contributors to the problem. Our coaches really focus on parent behavior in preseason parent meetings, and help parents to realize that what they do and say is huge. We try to help parents understand that their kids play sports mostly to have fun. If parents will listen to their kids, they will hear some very interesting things. Most of the time the very thing parents are trying to do, offer advice to improve their children's performance, is actually hurting the children the most by making them nervous and anxious and sometimes embarrassed.

Let it be clear from the beginning that parents should always be the primary and most important teachers of values to their children. Schools, though, have a role in the process of teaching shared values of fair play, honesty, and integrity.

It's not happening that way in our schools, and there's a reason. The requirements of No Child Left Behind, which place a heavy burden on schools for their students to perform well on standardized tests, have resulted in a focus on math and reading for the purposes of testing.

In recent years, there's been an influx of non-English speaking students into our schools. They may be second graders or seniors; it doesn't matter when they arrived—they have to meet the NCLB requirements. For these students, it means more instruction in English to prepare for them for the all-important tests at the year's end.

More and more students come from single-parent homes or homes with two working parents. Many of these students move frequently, both within and out of the school district. In order to keep your job, you, the teacher, must teach them math and reading. Students who change school districts may face pressure to score at a certain level, particularly at schools that are in danger in losing funding due to poor scores.

It's all about the tests. At least, that's what many believe. The Associated Press and AOL partnered in January 2006 to commission a poll on parents' and teachers' attitudes regarding No Child Left Behind.

"Virtually every parent I know feels the schools are educating to the two subjects they are testing," said Mitchell Stiers, an Iowa father of three, in the AP report on the poll results.

The threat of legal action has also damped efforts toward character-based education and discipline. In 2004, Public Agenda and Common Good took a close look at what's been going on in American classrooms.

In *Teaching Interrupted*, a story about the report, the *Washington Post* reported that 49 percent of the teachers polled said that they'd been accused of unfairly disciplining a student, and 55 percent believe that school districts are contributing to the problem by knuckling under to the complaining parents of student troublemakers. An astonishing 78 percent said there were students in their classrooms who needed to be removed from the normal classroom setting.

Two Montgomery, Alabama, teachers found themselves in the local jail after a parent pressed charges against the pair for their role in breaking up a lunchroom brawl. The charges were dismissed, but the damage has been done. Educators' fears about disciplining students is real. I can't say that I blame them; they have to feed their families. Is it worth losing your job to teach a child proper behavior?

The Public Agenda and Common Good report shows that such incidents have created a culture in which teachers ignore problems and choose not to get involved. Talk about wasted teaching opportunities!

We're missing opportunities every day. The bottom line is, children will learn from someone who's willing to teach them. Often, that person is a coach not affiliated with the school. This is troubling.

Granted, I'm oversimplifying the landscape of our schools. There are many more issues that administrators, teachers, and coaches face every day, making their task monumental. I've spent a great deal of time with hundreds of administrators, teachers, and coaches, and I remain shocked by what they must deal with on a regular basis.

With that in mind, think back to how you learned about sportsmanship. Maybe your father, mother, or older brother explained, in a teachable moment, a desirable behavior trait like, when you hit a home run against your next-door neighbor, you shouldn't make fun of him while you run the bases, because you wouldn't want him to do that to you.

Or maybe your youth coach explained that no matter whether we win or lose, we're going to shake the other team's hands and congratulate them and thank them for a good game.

I learned about lying in the eighth grade. This story is less about the teachable moment than about the fact that, at age forty, I still remember the day, the event, the embarrassment, and the feeling of shame in my gut. I remember The Lesson.

My teammates and I were running wind sprints at the end of football practice. I was tired. So was everyone else. I decided to loaf but did my best to make it look like I was trying. My coach knew what I was doing and gave me a chance to redeem myself on the last gasser. I didn't, and because of me the entire team had to run ten more. My teammates were all over me.

Afterward, the coach pulled me aside and asked me why I hadn't tried harder when both he and I knew I obviously was not giving it my all. I said I was tired and thought I could get away with it. He took the time to explain to me what honor and integrity meant, and that the rest of the team looked up to me, so if I displayed this kind of behavior, then they would as well.

What if that coach had chosen not to do that with me because he was afraid my dad would complain to the administration? Why should a coach or a teacher or school administration have to worry about frivolous lawsuits in the pursuit of acceptable discipline? But they do, and that's what alarms me in my travels across the country and discussions with coaches and educators.

As a result, I'm seeing fewer and fewer schools and coaches teaching or enforcing sportsmanlike behavior. From what we've seen through our nationwide research, most of the coaches want their players to display good sportsmanship, but many are afraid to really enforce that behavior and make it a priority in their teaching process. Can you blame them?

Sports are such a great metaphor for life; they afford educators a great opportunity to solve classroom problems. Take bullying, for example, and let's look at the primary grade levels K–5. Our research shows that many bullying instances take place outside the classroom, during recess and PE.

When a teacher is teaching and students are sitting at their desks, there's little opportunity for a bullying incident. But when those kids get out of class and onto the playground or in physical education, that's when bullying manifests. A non-athletic third grader is pushed around by the larger, more athletic boy, or the new girl is told she can't play with the more well-established group of girl friends. That's where it starts, and many of us never forget those scars from that young age.

This is where sportsmanship education should begin and can be incredibly powerful. Teaching young students to put themselves in the other person's shoes and understand their feelings can have a dramatic impact on a young person. But it's not about just telling them; we have to use real scenarios and allow students to see and feel the real consequences of their actions. Sports are perfectly suited to these types of lessons. In heated sporting events, no matter whether they're organized games or the pick-up variety, when the games get to the last inning or the last twenty seconds, a person's true character — child or adult — is revealed.

In 2005, the State of Alabama purchased our company's STAR Sportsmanship program for every fourth-grade classroom in the state. As part of the program, students were administered a pretest on sportsmanship. The feedback we received proved shocking to the teachers:

"They seemed to want to be mean."

"Their parents would be shocked to see some of their answers."

"Where are they learning this? From TV?"

Here's an example from the pretest:

**Scenario 1:** Imagine that you're playing in the most important basketball game of your life. The winner of today's game will play for the league championship. There are only twenty seconds left, and your team is behind by one point.

The referee blows the whistle and says you stepped out of bounds. You know you did not. What will you do?

   a. *Don't say anything about the call that you think is unfair, and continue playing.*

   b. *Give the referee an angry look so he won't call you out of bounds next time.*

   c. *Tell your teammates the referee is unfair.*

   d. *Explain to the referee that you didn't step out of bounds.*

Most of the students chose "d"—a statement of complaint or explanation to the official that they hadn't stepped out of bounds.

The answers were crafted to determine whether nine- and ten-year-olds believed it was okay to challenge the ruling of the authority figure, in this case the official. The problem is, that attitude often manifests itself in more defiant behavior at age eighteen.

Take a moment to ponder this test question and think back to when you were ten. I remember being scared of the referees. There was no way that I would talk to them. If they blew the whistle and said you were out of bounds, then you got ready to play defense. If our ten-year-olds think it's okay to "explain" to the referee that in fact *he* is wrong and made a mistake, what happens later in life when they get a call they think is wrong? I guess they spit in the umpire's face!

The yearlong pilot yielded very interesting results. Of the entire fourth-grade population we received pre- and post-test results for more than 5,000 students—one of the largest sportsmanship studies ever conducted in the US. There was a 22 percent increase in knowledge gained by these students after using the STAR program. The comments from teachers and coaches were also very interesting.

47

They were amazed at how "mean" the kids' responses seemed to be. As they questioned their students further, it became apparent that poor sportsmanship was not only impacting the kids' self-esteem and other aspects of their lives, but also reducing the educators' ability to teach and to improve scores on math and reading tests.

Many of the behavior issues in a school revolve around athletics. For example, think back to physical education class, recess, organized youth sports, and the locker room just before heading out to practice. Numerous bullying incidents take place in these settings. The kid who can't throw as well as others is mocked. Coaches and teachers have a responsibility to help every student understand the consequences of his or her actions and how their cruel words make others feel. It's pretty simple but it's often overlooked.

Barry Mano, of the National Association of Sports Officials and *Referee Magazine,* points out that "people are less willing to accept anything they perceive as an injustice. They want redress for their grievances."

That's how court actions are filed seeking to overturn game results due to officials' calls and administrators' actions regarding eligibility. No one wants to lose.

Coaches have an important role, but let's not diminish the role of the entire education community. It takes an all-out, focused effort by every teacher, coach, principal, superintendent, and parent to educate our kids on good sportsmanship. Done properly, it will actually help educators do a better job of improving test scores. How? We're now seeing research from this same study that students are returning from recess and PE with fewer behavior issues and prepared to learn sooner. Teachers are becoming more comfortable with the STAR methodology; they can quickly remind their students of it to help them get ready to begin their classroom studies without delay.

The best-behaved are usually the best students, and they're the ones who do better on the standardized tests. Investment in character education pays dividends in the short term for the classroom and in the long term for life.

## Chapter Six

# Coaching to Win the Biggest Game of All—Life

I've never served in the armed forces. Had I done so, I would surely have been a marine. Why? Because Gene Andrews was a marine—forgive me—*is* a marine.

Little things meant a lot to my high school football coach. In his view, if you were sloppy about the little things, then you'd be sloppy about the big ones. If you were satisfied with less than your best effort on a seemingly inconsequential play during a game, then you were likely to make a mistake at a critical time. If you were lackadaisical when your team was up 35-0, what experience would you draw upon when your team was down 14-10 in the final minute?

Win at all costs? Quite the opposite. Like everyone else who's ever set foot on the playing field, Gene Andrews wanted to win. Victory, though, wasn't worth much if it was achieved by cutting corners, breaking rules, and not handling oneself with dignity and honor. In Gene's eyes, losing a game but maintaining those principals was a far higher achievement. Because of his steadfast adherence to those ideas, his teams developed a certain work ethic, and because of his and his team's commitment to that work ethic, losses with honor were few, and victories obtained the right way were many.

"After going to Vietnam, you appreciated the little things when you got back," Andrews told me.

My children hear my voice every day, but they're actually hearing a little of Gene Andrews in my voice. "Tuck in your shirt." Why does it matter to me? Because it mattered to Coach Andrews. In the scheme of life, one can argue that a shirttail is seemingly inconsequential. But the shirttail, while obviously a little thing, is the first step in establishing discipline. Wearing a shirttail untucked sends a message. Worrying about it shows a concern for the little things.

"I just always believed that you could behave like an officer and a gentleman, so to speak," Andrews said.

In Gene Andrews's eyes, and in mine due to his influence, taking care of the little things better prepares you for the big ones. I'm not talking about the game against your fiercest rival. Rather, I'm talking about what happens for our children beyond their playing days. The discipline instilled in life through parents, teachers, coaches — through all role models — will provide the foundation on which today's children make life decisions.

At the time, we, the football team, thought Coach A was a bit "over the top," but I remember my father, also a marine, telling me that Coach was absolutely right. That confirmation from another role model helped me accept, embrace, and now teach those same principles.

The challenge many coaches face today is that they may be the *only ones* teaching these principles. Single-parent homes, lack of parental understanding of the issue, unwillingness to accept that maybe your child could use some discipline, and a host of other issues are making it increasingly difficult for today's coach.

It's easily proven that we live in a world hungry for instant gratification. Sadly, that's partnered with a lowering of expectations.

While parents clearly are the main influence in building a value system in children, the children's behavior in sport is more influenced by their coaches.

John Wooden, arguably the greatest coach who's ever lived, has told the story scores of times of how he'd spend the first practice session with his UCLA teams. It would be a painstaking, stepwise process on how to put on socks and shoes! The littlest of things garnered the most attention.

While I wasn't a basketball player, and am too young to have played for Coach Wooden, I was fortunate enough to play for a pretty good coach myself. By the time I arrived at Auburn University, having transferred from the University of Tennessee, Coach Pat Dye had been on the job for five years. He had played for Wally Butts at the University of Georgia from 1958–1960 and had been a coach from the day he was released from military service. He coached for Paul "Bear" Bryant at the University of Alabama for several years before becoming head coach at East Carolina in 1974. Upon my arrival, Coach Dye had been coaching for twenty years and had been head coach for ten. He wasn't even fifty—which seems much younger these days than I recall it seeming twenty years ago—but he was an experienced coach. He knew what he was doing, and I learned a lot from him.

Coach Dye didn't tolerate foolishness from his players. He would disagree with officials—sometimes vehemently. He let us know it was his job to communicate with the officials, not ours. Captains could call time-outs and accept or decline penalties. The rest of the talking was to be done by him.

In 1987, we were playing Florida State at Jordan-Hare Stadium in Auburn. It was the classic example of a game in which nothing went right. We came into the game a top-five team nationally, with a 7-0-1 record, and Florida State was an outstanding team, too. At one point, we were backed up against our goal line when fourth down arose. I went in to punt.

Florida State has a reputation for blocking punts with great regularity. They had ten men lined up to come after the punt—and me, the punter.

It was no easy chore. If I managed to get the ball away, then it meant that Deion Sanders would return the punt, and Deion was the most exciting punt returner in the country.

True to its reputation, Florida State put on a heavy rush. I felt a tiny bit of contact after the punt. Sadly, I decided to become an actor: I flopped to the ground as if I'd been shot with a deer rifle. My performance wasn't worthy of an Academy Award. The referee ignored me and watched the play continue. Coach Dye exploded from the sideline. He lit into the officials, protesting the non-call. About 70,000 Auburn fans were booing from the stands. I jogged over to the sideline and was met immediately by Coach Dye, who'd stopped his tirade long enough to ask me a critical question: "Did they rough you?" I shook my head quickly no, and that was it. Not another peep from Coach. If there was a penalty, he'd make his voice heard, but he wasn't about to lie to try to influence the officials or to rile up the crowd.

It was a valuable lesson that stays with me today, because coaches influence the way we look at games and, to a great extent, at life itself. Why should we be surprised that a National Association of Sports Officials survey showed that nearly two out of three respondents said the coach has the biggest impact on sportsmanship? It's no surprise at all.

Teams assume the personality of their coaches, after all. When the coach won't tolerate poor sportsmanship, then it doesn't take place. It's simple. If the coach has the guts to stop it, and the administration has the guts to back him or her, then it stops.

A book that captures the essence of what coaches should be is *Coaching for Character* by Craig Clifford and Randolph Feezell.

I had an opportunity to interview Craig Clifford and discuss the work that he and Randolph Feezell did in their book. Clifford introduced the fact that in order for there to be a game there must be a worthy opponent. If I were covering Terrel Owens and he scored, it wouldn't be much of an accomplishment. Therefore, all of us should respect our opponents. This is obvious, yet the actions of the players on the field, and the parents and fans in the stand, indicate a completely opposite understanding.

After the Packers released me, I was offered an opportunity to coach full-time. I'd had such a great experience with my coaches, and recognized the tremendous positive influence they'd had on my life, so it really appealed to me. Ultimately, I didn't choose to be a full-time coach, but during that process I thought about why I wanted to coach and immediately thought back to Coach Andrews, Coach Dye, Coach Paul Davis, special-teams coach at Auburn, and others. A few questions came to mind, questions I hadn't thought about since that time. Then I read Clifford and Feezell's book and interviewed

Clifford. The questions they posed to coaches are similar to some that I thought through as well.

Will the players you're coaching today want their kids to come back and play for you?

I know I'd want my children to play for Coach Andrews, Coach Dye, and Coach Davis. They set a high standard to live up to, and it has nothing to do with wins and losses, but everything to do with the men they are and the life lessons they taught me.

If I decide to coach, how do I want to be remembered by my players? Who are the coaches I respect most?

I knew that if I was going to be a coach and be successful I had to have the right answers to those questions. Clifford and Feezell pose similar questions, and really get a coach thinking about what's important and the foundation of his or her coaching philosophy.

I have tremendous respect for my high school and college coaches, and, of course, Coach Wooden. His team-first philosophy would stand out in today's look-at-me world. I remember hearing on TV that famed North Carolina basketball coach Dean Smith required any of his players who'd just scored a basket to point to the player who'd passed him the ball or set a screen. The point was a thank-you for the player who'd made the sacrifice, an acknowledgment by the player who'd scored that he couldn't have done it alone.

There's an inherent conflict in the coach's job description: He's expected to be a teacher of the game, a molder of character, *and* have a winning record. On many occasions, it's tough to accomplish two of those tasks, let alone all three. To use the game as a teaching tool for life, winning must sometimes take a back seat to the other two tasks. A few more coaching-related questions will get us to the heart of it:

- *Do you ever yell at your players?*

- *Do you berate officials? What about in a really big game?*

- *Do you allow trash-talking by your players?*

For sportsmanship to live, we must build strategies that help coaches be able to truthfully answer no to all of those; the magnitude of the game shouldn't matter.

"Of course I yell at players and officials," you might answer.

Granted, there are circumstances in which players should be chastised, and occasions when the officials must be informed of situations on the field that they might be unaware of. But realize that when you make a continual habit of yelling at the officials, you're telling your players that it's always open season on officials. And when you constantly yell at your players, you're teaching them to continually berate subordinates.

It's a horrible message to teach our youth.

A parent has the best opportunity to develop a child's behavior at home, at school, and almost everywhere else, but one place where parents aren't the primary influence is on the playing field. That's where coaches are the key influence and have the best opportunity to send a new message.

Certain situations require extra attention from coaches. Officials will tell you that there are more problems on the field in lopsided games as one team gets increasingly frustrated at its lack of success, and the winning team shows up its rivals with various embarrass actions.

Coaches have the responsibility to try to win games within the rules. Once the game's outcome is no longer in doubt, coaches must use the experience as a teaching tool regardless of whether they're the winning or the losing team. They must police the behavior of their players to ensure a safe conclusion to the game, so all can walk away with their dignity intact.

If coaches get sucked into the "let's have fun because we're winning by four touchdowns" mentality, or the "we can't win the game, so we might as well win the fight" mindset, they fail their players and society miserably.

Put simply, coaches in youth leagues should never encourage or allow their players to:

- *Run up the score;*

- *Talk trash to their opponents;*

- *Do anything to belittle their opponents;*

- *Try to injure another player;*

- *Intentionally break the rules.*

Last season, a California high school football coach found himself jobless after an incident caught on video tape in which he was moving the down markers to benefit his team.

That, of course, is the extreme, but we'd be naive to think that coaches don't make the mistakes listed above. When they do, they're teaching our children to be cheaters and poor sports.

Coaches, it's this simple: If there's to be a change in our young people's sports behavior, the change must begin in you and come from you. They won't change until you demand it of them.

There are strategies that coaches can embrace to change a child's mindset and help foster a rebirth of sportsmanship.

In my interview with Clifford, he introduced a fantastic concept: Let's change our view of a player's "talent." It's not a talent, but a "gift," something the athlete has been blessed with. It must be cherished, nurtured, and protected because it's temporary in nature. Help them understand that the "gift" is a part of them that was presented to them, not necessarily earned.

Think of yourself more as a teacher than as a coach. Teach character and sportsmanship every day, just like you teach your sport skills.

Many youth coaches use sports—and the children playing them—to satisfy their own unfulfilled dreams. They set out to meet the children's needs, but end up spending a lot of time wondering what parents are thinking of them. All coaches deal with the potential conflict of interest in their duties: develop character and improve individual skills and still win.

How do coaches find perspective in youth sports? Look for opportunities to teach. If it's a priority to you, it'll be a priority to your team. Use positive reinforcement liberally. After all, it's what kids are looking for. They want and need healthy self-esteem.

The coach's first job is to like his players and show them that he does, regardless of their performance. Don't misunderstand me: I'm not calling for a lack of discipline. The application of discipline is an expression of love and respect from parent to child and from coach to player. So, discipline early and often. Teach early and often.

Every season should begin with a meeting for players, parents, and coaches. Outline the expectations you have for the players and for the parents.

Don't be afraid to tell parents not to yell at their children during games. Ask them to cheer for their children, but tell them you expect them not to coach from the stands.

Tell parents that their child's worth—and their worth as parents—isn't determined by how many points their child scores. Tell them that the game is for the children, not for the parents to relive childhood memories.

Build a philosophy that gives every player an active role on the team.

There may be times during the season when you have to ask parents to modify their behavior. This should occur when a parent:

1. *continually coaches from the stands;*

2. *focuses on their child's mistakes; or*

3. *reprimands their child in front of others for mistakes made in competition.*

Ask them politely to change their behavior, and hopefully they'll understand your expectations.

Occasionally, parents will ask to see you and ask questions of you. Allow them their say. Make sure that they've fully aired their grievances, and make any changes you deem reasonable. Coaches have to police their own behavior to make sure they're meeting their own expectations.

A solid exercise for any coach to go through prior to a season is to take a sheet of paper and write down what you'll do to win a game, to make the playoffs, and to win a championship.

Several years ago the Minnesota Amateur Sports Commission conducted a study that revealed how coaches had treated their young athletes:

- *45.3 percent of the youngsters surveyed said they'd been called names.*

- *21 percent said they were pressured to play with an injury.*

- *17.5 percent said they'd been hit, kicked, or slapped.*

- *8.2 percent said they had been pressured to intentionally harm others.*

This means that we have a ways to go, but we have the path to bring back sportsmanship. Coach, on the practice field and on the playing field, you have the best chance to make it happen.

John Stewart, executive director of the Florida High School Athletic Association, runs one of the nation's largest public school athletic systems. His background is education administration. His forty-year career went from the classroom to the principal's office to a superintendent's office to becoming Deputy Commissioner of Education for the State of Florida. Three years ago, he went to the FHSAA. He's hired a few coaches in his time.

"I would almost want to hire them on the spot if they told me that they wanted to develop youngsters and make them young men and women instead of athletes," Stewart said. "That's the necessary attitude."

Stewart agrees with those who say that coaches must step away from the heat of the moment.

"Coaches need to treat children the way they would want their children to be treated," he said. "Understand that each youngster is a special human being."

Stewart says coaching offers a wonderful opportunity to teach.

"Parents are the first and best teachers of sportsmanship," he said. "But there is a time when the coach has the most influence on certain behavior. Athletes, particularly young males, will run through brick walls for their coaches."

And athletes will emulate their coaches, which, according to Dan Washburn, executive director of the Alabama High School Athletic Association, can be troublesome. Washburn is also completing his term as president of the National Federation of State High School Athletic Associations.

Washburn found one Friday night in the fall of 2005 particularly disturbing. Fifty-one players and coaches were ejected on this night. Players are ejected for fighting, flagrant acts, or foul language. Coaches, by rule, are ejected after their second unsportsmanlike-conduct penalty.

"It's occurring at an alarming rate," Washburn said. "We have roughly 200 games on a Friday night, and to have fifty-one ejections is a huge disappointment."

That night has resulted in a renewed commitment to sportsmanship. A new initiative with Learning Through Sports is under way, coupled with a new discipline program. Washburn said, "We had a fine system, but I think people didn't view it as severe. It is now. Things that were costing schools $250 could cost $1,500. That will get the attention of administrators and coaches. No doubt, it's a big leap. But it's important."

Washburn makes an excellent point when he says that student athletes aren't the only ones affected by media images. "Coaches see what coaches do on television," he said. "Baseball coaches see how the big-league managers act up. It's not appropriate for high school coaches. Our coaches must understand that not every day and every game is going to be blue skies."

Grant Teaff, Executive Director of the American Football Coaches Association and former head football coach at Baylor University, has always made a case for sportsmanship in football. Coach Teaff uses a quote from the poem by Edgar A. Guess to remind the AFCA membership of their responsibility to practice what they preach. The quote: "I'd rather see a sermon than to hear one any day...." It clearly makes the point to coaches that teaching everyday values are extremely important; coaches must exhibit what they teach in their own behavior.

Coach Teaff points to the 1994 season as a turning point for sportsmanship on the football field. "Fighting on the field during the 1994 season rose to epidemic proportions," he said. "At our meeting of Division 1-A head coaches in January 1995, everyone was disgusted with what had taken place during the previous season." The coaches came out of the meeting with a mandate for the NCAA Football Rules committee: "Do what it takes to stop outbreaks of fighting on the football field."

"Working with the Football Rules committee, we developed a video that showed proper sportsmanlike conduct and implemented more rules that would keep players from drawing attention to themselves through unsportsmanlike conduct," Teaff said. "The stronger rules worked beautifully, and the greater emphasis has had a very positive effect on the game of football."

Teaff went on to say, "Two years ago, the NCAA held a summit calling on presidents, athletic directors, head football coaches, and officials to intensify their effort to make sportsmanship an important part of the college-game experience. The efforts on individual campuses paid great dividends, not only in teaching student-athletes the importance of sportsmanship, but carrying it to the student body and to the fans and asking for their support as well.

"Even though the NFL has made some aggressive strides toward sportsmanship, they still have a ways to go. When youth and high school football players watch some of their favorite NFL heroes bring attention to themselves by talking on a cell phone after a score, or competing for the most unusual gyration after a tackle, sack, or touchdown, it sends the wrong message and thus becomes an ongoing problem for college football as well.

"We, parents, fans, coaches, players, and officials must work together to teach the importance of sportsmanship and the value it brings to the game itself."

How can coaches and administrators turn the corner? They would be wise to encourage and model what's going to boost sportsmanship. Ronnie Carter, executive director of the Tennessee Secondary Schools Athletic Association, has instituted groundbreaking programs in this area.

First, when a school is fined by the TSSAA, the money goes to the A. F. Bridges program. A. F. Bridges was one of the forefathers of high school athletics in Tennessee. His name adorns a sportsmanship award for Tennessee athletes, and more important, a scholarship program.

"We started out with fines when there were problems, but we quickly learned that it was going to take more than that," Carter said. "It was going to take a positive approach."

The answer was sportsmanship awards for schools that display the best attitude, and scholarships to male and female athletes in each classification for their sportsmanship.

"This wasn't about giving prizes to the school that finished in last place," he said. "It is geared to honor those who are doing right."

Carter acknowledges it warms his heart to see *Bridges* banners hanging next to championship banners in Tennessee gymnasiums.

Football holds a special place in Tennessee, as it does in other parts of the country. With larger crowds and larger rosters, football requires extra care and planning when it comes to sportsmanship and security. Carter developed an initiative that helps build a positive approach. Approximately fifteen minutes before kickoff, before the captains meet for the coin toss, another meeting takes place. Participating are the officials, the head coaches, and the administrators in charge for both schools.

"It's basically a meeting where everyone goes over their roles—their responsibilities at the game," Carter said. "It's not adversarial. It's an opportunity for the host team, which runs the meeting, to say, 'We're glad you've come to our house tonight.' It sets the right tone."

At the same time, the public address announcer informs the audience of the subject of the meeting and presents a public service announcement regarding sportsmanship.

"It dovetails with our sportsmanship program and everything we're trying to do," Carter said.

The Tennessee meeting is a prime example of people working together to head off potential problems and take a proactive approach to sportsmanship. It would be wise to emulate the Tennessee program in every state.

Coach Teaff had it right regarding the sermon. Coach, you must talk to your players about sportsmanship. But if you're not showing it, then your words are empty.

# Redefining a Metaphor for Life

I love how Barry Mano sums up youth-league sports.

"It is the intersection of the least experienced players, the least experienced coaches, and the least experienced officials."

To add to Mano's thoughts, it's also where the deepest emotions are. Those aren't professionals out there—those are our kids. We want them to succeed. It's when we want them to succeed to make us look successful that we create problems.

We must remember that for children to succeed in life, they must understand the concepts of victory and defeat, of teamwork and sacrifice, that life is a journey, and not everyone gets to be the guy who scores touchdowns or the girl who shoots the winning basket.

Sports have been wonderful to me. I've found role models, mentors, and friends, and I have great memories that I'll cherish until I die. And even though my dream of punting in the NFL didn't unfold the way I'd hoped, I had the opportunity. Below is a letter that my late father wrote to me while I was a walk-on at the University of Tennessee, where I tried and failed before playing at Auburn. The letter is valuable because at the time I couldn't see beyond what had happened in the last practice, or what I'd be up against in the next practice, as I tried to win a starting job in the SEC. I just knew that I wasn't starting, and I wanted to, and it frustrated me. My father took the time to put into words some very powerful concepts that, looking back, I can so much more easily understand. First of all, he was telling me that he was proud of my effort and attitude.

Then he explained that true growth as a human being is what happens during the journey. Real growth isn't the victory or defeat or how good your punting average is. That's hard for even an adult to accept, but it's true.

Think back for a moment about Gayle Sayers and Brian Piccolo, Jackie Robinson, Jim Abbott, and Jim Valvano. The list goes on and on; there are thousands of exemplary players and coaches who had the right perspective. Some were great and won championships or set records. But what we remember most about these guys and girls was how they played or coached the game. That's the lesson we need to teach our players, their parents, and our coaches.

Will the opportunity exist for our children and for our children's children? The question is legitimate because if we don't get a handle on what's happening on a regular basis on our playing fields and in the stands, we may lose one of life's greatest gifts—the ability to play.

For all practical purposes, sportsmanship is dead. But the athletes are better, and sports are more popular than ever, and I know we can breathe new life into sportsmanship by building and insisting upon a culture of teamwork, fair play, and mutual respect. All of us have a special role to play in reviving sportsmanship.

If we do this, sports can again become a positive metaphor for life that we can all enjoy.

Dear Son,

Even though I talk to you every day, I feel maybe at this time it's best to write you a letter that may be helpful to you; that during the times you feel depressed or frustrated you can read over, and by seeing the truth gain impetus to continue in this endeavor.

The last time I sent you a letter was many years ago when you were at FRA football camp for the first time for a week. If you can recollect the many anxieties you felt then, it could be helpful now with the many anxieties you feel at this time.

Coping with anxiety is very difficult, but the only way a human being can grow with strength and build character is to struggle with each anxiety to overcome those feelings. When you overcome them, you learn the true meaning of living. Many people do not want to fight those anxieties and try to understand them. Without fighting them, they escape, and you never grow.

I believe if you really think about what I'm saying now, you'll get the full meaning of living. Along with the pain and hurt, we also have happiness. It's not all black and white. There are mixed feelings, and while you're struggling to obtain your desired goal, you're also feeling fulfillment and self-esteem. Knowing that you're taking on this challenge with no guarantee of the outcome will build strength and character. With each day, you're growing stronger and stronger emotionally, and this is the way you become an emotionally mature person, Brian.

Don't look back, don't evaluate the others; you have an objective—strive for that. By not looking behind, you won't create your own fears and plant negative feelings about yourself in your own mind. By concentrating only on yourself, you won't allow your mind to wander, for when it does, it will automatically pick up negatives about your own worth.

You must discipline your thinking to stay within yourself because human beings all feel a certain amount of inadequacy, lack of self-worth. The only way a person can overcome these feelings is to concentrate by disciplining your mind to think of what you're doing. Concentrate totally on your objective, and that will prevent negative feelings from entering it. Just think positive thoughts, and it will end up positive. Don't think of the future, because it can create negatives; don't think of the past (like all the hard work you've done). Thinking of the future can create negatives since it is unknown. Thinking of the past is a negative because we think we deserve something. Think only of here and now, and that will help you grow in your ability to accomplish what you want. If you concentrate on the here and now, you can't receive any negative feelings because your concentration is on the immediate; you're not allowing for any distractions, and therefore you must grow.

Here's how you must grow—you gain more strength in your abilities, more strength in your character, and definitely more worth as a human being. Brian, if this is too deep, let's talk about it and maybe I can explain it verbally one-on-one. Even though words are easily said, and deeds are hard to accomplish, if you can train your mind to think these thoughts, you must grow and feel more satisfied within you.

The outcome of this kind of thinking is tremendous self-confidence. You're an extremely bright person, and I know you can accomplish this. I've seen you do these things before, that's why I know you can. I want you to know that I'm extremely proud of you for entering this challenge, and while I understand it's difficult to cope with each day, which is normal for anybody, to stick with it as you are is enough for me to feel very proud to call you son.

> *Love,*
> *Dad*